# JESUS
# THE FILLER OF OUR NEEDS
# IDENTITY

BY RICK SIZEMORE

*Jesus, The Filler of Our Needs Workbook: Identity - How to Live in the Fullness of Who You Really Are*
Copyright © 2022 by Rick Sizemore

All rights reserved. No part of this publication may be reproduced, stored in or introduced into a retrieval system, or transmitted, in any form, or by any means, (electronic, mechanical, photocopying, recording, or otherwise), without the prior written permission of both the copyright owner and the above publisher of this book.

The scanning, uploading, and distribution of this book via the Internet or via any other means without the permission of the publisher is illegal and punishable by law. Please purchase only authorized electronic editions, and do not participate in or encourage electronic piracy of copyrighted materials. Your support of the author's rights is appreciated.

Unless otherwise indicated, Scripture quotations are taken from the New American Standard Bible®, Copyright © 1960, 1962, 1963, 1968, 1971, 1972, 1973, 1975, 1977, 1995 by The Lockman Foundation. Used by permission. (www.Lockman.org)

Where marked NKJV, Scripture is taken from the New King James Version®. Copyright © 1982 by Thomas Nelson. Used by permission. All rights reserved.

The author has chosen to emphasize certain words or phrases in Scripture quotations. The emphases (in bold) are his own.

Where applicable, names have been changed to protect privacy.

For more information on books and other products by Rick Sizemore,
please visit: **www.ricksizemore.org** or **www.dealingjesus.org**

Published and produced by:

Tall Wood Publishing House
PO Box 8
Pembroke, Virginia 24136

Cover & Interior Design by BookBloks.com

Paperback ISBN: 978-1-57688-096-8
eBook ISBN: 978-1-57688-097-5

Printed in the United States of America

# TABLE OF CONTENTS

Introduction .................................................................................. v

    Chapter 1: Who Am I? *Experiencing the Fullness of Who You Are* ...................... 1

    Chapter 2: The Identity of God ................................................................ 7

    Chapter 3: Benefits of Our Identity in Jesus ........................................... 13

    Chapter 4: Symptoms of the Need for Identity ....................................... 17

    Chapter 5: How to Satisfy the Need for Identity .................................... 23

    Chapter 6: Obstacles to Accepting Our Identity in Jesus ........................ 29

    Chapter 7: The Fullness of Identity ........................................................ 35

    Chapter 8: Working It Out *Reestablishing Your Identity in Jesus* ................ 41

The Fullness of Christ ................................................................... 63

Bibliography ................................................................................ 65

Notes .......................................................................................... 67

# INTRODUCTION

When I was younger, I struggled to know who I was. My "identity" seemed to be compromise, selfishness, and instability. I often hurt the people who were closest to me, and I unknowingly tried to destroy the gifts God wanted to give me. I needed the fullness of Jesus in my life and didn't realize it. Many of the needs mentioned in this workbook went unmet inside me, and I had no idea. Consequently, I acted out of deep need on a daily basis.

As I have grown in my relationship with God and processed many of the negative events I endured, I can tell you with certainty that my life has changed in dramatic ways. Because of the fullness of Jesus, I am a different person now.

The truth is that God meets all our needs. That is how He made us—so He could be the One to comfort us, bring healing, and lead us into being who we really are. As we are filled with the reality of Jesus, our needs are not "needs" anymore, but they become places of fullness and expressions of God's goodness in our life.

This workbook is based on my book *Jesus: The Filler of Our Needs*, which talks about the nine soulish needs the mind and heart require in order to function in a healthy way: love, identity, acceptance, worth, intimacy, purpose, security, forgiveness, and the need to be needed.[1] This workbook explains the nine needs more thoroughly and how they can operate in a person's life. I recommend reading *Jesus: The Filler of Our Needs*; however, you do not have to read that book before completing this workbook.

## WHAT DOES IT MEAN FOR JESUS TO MEET OUR NEEDS?

Here is a quick review of *Jesus: The Filler of Our Needs*:

1. **God created everything and every person in such a way that we *need* Jesus.** He is the One who holds everything together, and He has first place in everything; He is the divine Filler of all things everywhere (Colossians 1:16–20). In the beginning, Adam and Eve experienced the fullness of God in the Garden of Eden.

---

[1] The soul is the essence of who we are. These nine needs exist at the core of every person.

2. **Sin and death created needs (lack) in the human heart.** When Adam and Eve disobeyed God, it released the effects of sin and death into them, their immediate descendants, and all of mankind (Romans 5:12). As humans, we were cut off from the fullness of God, and the nine needs began to manifest in our life. (Genesis 3–4 tells the story.)

3. **Jesus is our Redeemer who saves us from the effects of sin and death.** Because of Jesus, we have the opportunity to *reverse* the effects of sin and death, and once more we get to experience the fullness of God in our soul (Colossians 1:19–22; 2:9–10). Jesus is the ultimate reservoir of grace that contains all of God's fullness. As we receive His fullness, the nine needs inside us are completely, wonderfully satisfied (Philippians 4:19).

4. **Jesus Christ is the only source that can abundantly meet all our needs.** Whenever Scripture talks about something being our *hope*, it means that thing is our source for life (see 1 Timothy 6:17; Colossians 1:27). That is what Jesus is—our hope of glory. If we try to get our needs met in other places, we invite trouble into our life. No source or hope other than Jesus can bring us fulfillment.

5. **Faith allows us to experience what we are hoping for.** Faith looks like believing and trusting. We *believe* God when He gives us a promise; that promise becomes our hope.[2] We *trust* Him by "attaching" our heart to His nature and character. Who He is becomes our hope the same way the promise is our hope.

6. When we "plug" ourselves into a certain hope through belief or trust, the resources of that hope are released into our life. When we believe God's Word, we are able to experience the fullness of His Word—Jesus. As we trust Him, our life is filled to overflowing with all His fullness, and our needs are met in abundant ways.

7. **Through faith we experience the conduits of Heaven.** The fullness of Jesus flows into us through three sources:

    - God's Word (Matthew 4:4),
    - The body of Christ (Ephesians 1:22–23), and
    - The Person of the Holy Spirit (John 7:37–39).

    As we use one or all three of these conduits,[3] the beautiful, world-creating fullness of Jesus is allowed to flood our life.

8. **God is constantly pouring Jesus' fullness into our soul.** The act of "plugging" our faith into the hope of Jesus abundantly satisfies our soulish needs, including the need for identity, which is the subject of this workbook. When we are filled with Jesus' fullness, we cannot be stopped—a fact the devil knows very well.[4] His only recourse is to try to drain our heart of faith through unbelief, doubt, hardness of heart, and worry. Unfortunately, that is where much of the body of Christ is today. As we go through difficult

---

[2] One example of this is found in Genesis 15:5–6, where God made Abraham a promise, and Abraham believed Him. "He reckoned it to him as righteousness."
[3] I use the word *conduit* with great respect, because God's Word, the body of Christ, and the Person of the Holy Spirit are precious gifts that have been given to us, so we can experience all the resources of Heaven (Ephesians 1:3).
[4] Being filled up with Jesus' fullness means being *more* than a conqueror. Not just somebody who can maybe conquer certain things, but someone who is *more* than what it takes to conquer things (1 John 5:4–5).

events designed by our adversary, we often find ourselves dealing with a lack of faith—even though the fullness of Jesus is right there and available to us.

9. **We are growing into Jesus' image.** As the children of God, we have a glorious destiny: growing into the image of Jesus (Romans 8:29). This involves Jesus becoming the fabric and content of our heart. God doesn't want us just to experience Jesus through the presence of the Holy Spirit, but He wants *the fullness of Jesus* to become the very composition of our heart, as well as everything inside our heart.[5]

Most of the time in a Christian's life, the fullness of Jesus simply and innocently fills our soul through the presence of the Holy Spirit, who helps us walk in His love, identity, acceptance, worth, intimacy, purpose, security, and forgiveness; He completely fills our need to be needed. Whenever this happens, it is like the Holy Spirit is *carrying* us.

But sometimes a particular need (or maybe multiple needs all at once) begins to manifest in our life. We don't know who we are, and we don't realize how very accepted we are because of Jesus. Every time this happens, it is an opportunity for His fullness to become part of our heart. There is a difference between being carried by the Spirit and being *changed* by the Spirit.[6]

At the start of Jesus' earthly ministry, He had an amazing experience where the Holy Spirit came upon Him in visible form, and God the Father Himself publicly declared identity and acceptance over Him. Luke 4:1 says that Jesus was gloriously filled with the Holy Spirit, but immediately after this encounter, the Spirit led Him into a wilderness, where the enemy tempted Him. There in the wilderness, what the Father had just declared over Jesus was validated. It wasn't just an encounter anymore—it became part of Jesus' heart.

A similar thing happened to Peter. On the day of Pentecost, he was baptized and filled with the Holy Spirit. This happened three more times in the days following. Peter boldly, confidently, and *honorably* represented the name of Jesus.[7] But not too long after this, something shifted in his heart, and he became afraid—to the point that he actually stepped into hypocrisy. It was so bad that Paul rebuked him in front of everyone.[8] Personally, I think that in the early days of the Church, Peter rode the waves of what God was doing; the Holy Spirit carried him in some pretty amazing ways. But eventually the time came for the fullness of Jesus to become bedrock in Peter's heart.

Like Peter, we have seasons when the Holy Spirit empowers us to flow in Jesus' likeness. We operate according to the fullness of His love, identity, acceptance, etc. But following these seasons, we will have opportunities to choose Jesus at a deeper level, and if we do, His fullness will be established in us. In that place of *His* fullness, we become perfect and complete and lack nothing, like James 1:2–4 talks about.

When we face an opportunity for Jesus' fullness to become part of our heart, we need to understand two important things. First is the revelation of who Jesus really is, because this tells us who *we* really are. Think of when God the Father spoke glory and honor over Jesus at His baptism and later on the Mount of Transfiguration; think of the words He used. (We'll talk more about this later.)

Second, we need to remove the things that keep our heart from receiving the truth about Jesus' identity (Hebrews 12:1–13). A lot of things can stand in the way. For example, let's say a young woman was abused by her dad for years.

---

[5] Christ, fully formed inside us (Galatians 4:19).
[6] The human heart is like a cup, and Jesus is like a river of water. He can completely fill us up—to the point of altering the cup's composition (see Ephesians 3:17; 1 Peter 3:15).
[7] You can read the story here: Acts 2:1–4; 4:8; 4:13, 31.
[8] You can read the story here: Galatians 2:11–14.

When her heavenly Father starts revealing the glory and truth of His love for her, it could be *hard* for her heart to embrace what He's saying. Certain obstacles stand in the way: past pain, maybe some unforgiveness issues, etc. But as she sets these obstacles aside, she can do what she couldn't do before and eagerly receive her Father's love.

When we really understand those eight truths—that we *need* Jesus, that faith is what allows us to live as God's children, that He is *constantly* pouring His fullness into us, and so forth—we will have hope in ways we've never had hope before. We won't stumble into the traps of unmet needs or be blown around in life. We will be steady and firm in our faith, and we will be able to keep our eyes on Jesus.

## COMMON OBSTACLES TO FAITH

However, walking in those eight truths isn't necessarily easy! Why not? Because certain things stand in our way. We will have trouble responding in faith when we struggle with any of the following issues:

**Issue 1: Jesus is not firmly our hope.** When Israel believed in their insecurities more than they believed in God, they ran into "trust problems." They began to see themselves the way the enemy described them, not the way God described them (Numbers 13:33). Our need for identity will be exposed whenever our hope is established in anything other than Jesus. The only life we have is found in Him (Galatians 2:20).

**Issue 2: We are hoping in someone or something other than Jesus.** Israel struggled with a need for security when they set their hope on other nations, not on God, to save them (Jeremiah 2:13–19). We will find ourselves struggling with this need whenever we set our hope on a job, a relationship, or something else to fulfill our needs rather than Jesus.

**Issue 3: We don't understand what we have in Jesus.** The Bible calls this a lack of knowledge (Hosea 4:6). The truth of God is beautiful, and it is available to us, but if we don't understand what it is or that it is *real*, we will struggle. One common example is when a fellow believer passes away. If a brother or sister in Christ dies, we don't need to mourn without hope, thinking they are gone forever. There is hope even in death for us—because of Jesus (1 Thessalonians 4:13). Another example is feeling alone in life because we grew up without parental love or an awareness of God's love. The truth of the matter is that God loves us unceasingly, and He will never leave us or forsake us, but if we don't *know that* deep in our heart, we could struggle with a need for love.

**Issue 4: We're in an environment of sin, death, and trauma.** When Jeremiah witnessed the destruction of his beloved city, Jerusalem, he was heartbroken. For a time, his need for security was right there on the surface, completely exposed (Lamentations 3:17–18). We, too, could struggle with a need for security when we have endured a loss, such as the death of a loved one. A difficult environment can puncture our hope and cause it to drain away, which exposes our need for security.

**Issue 5: We're dealing with "faith distractions."** This happened to Peter when he was walking on the water with Jesus. He saw the storm billowing all around him, began to doubt, and started to sink (Matthew 14:28–31). A "faith distraction" can influence our need for identity. One common distraction is hardship. Maybe we're working hard to complete an important project, and something goes wrong. This can expose our need for identity. "I can't believe this happened. Who am I? I just don't know anymore."

**Issue 6: We've embraced sinful words or thoughts.** Israel took on an identity of defeat when other people's opinions became more important to them than God's opinions (Numbers 14:1–4). This can expose our need for worth. "This person thinks I'm useless and no good at my job, and maybe they're right."

**Issue 7: We commit sinful actions.** Sin can play with our head and lead us to believe things that are not true. A biblical example of this is when Israel disobeyed and rejected Moses. God had chosen Moses to be the deliverer, but Israel didn't want him (Acts 7:37–39). When a person sins, they open the door to the need for identity. This happens all the time with premarital sex. It can cause one or both parties to believe they are dirty, "used," or unable to continue with their destiny.

**Issue 8: People are sinning against us.** When Israel rejected Moses, he ran away (Acts 7:25–29). Their sin hung over his head for decades, and when God came to get him because it was time to bring the people out of Egypt, Moses didn't believe he was a good choice. He basically told the Lord, "It would be better if you picked someone else."

When people sin against us, it can cause a host of needs in our life. Think about a dad who divorces the mother and abandons their child. That little child will likely grow up with unmet needs, such as the need for security.

In summary, your needs are fully, wonderfully met in Jesus. Here's how:

- God created you to *need* Jesus.
- Sin creates lack in your heart, but Jesus the Redeemer saves you from the effects of sin. He is the only One who can abundantly meet *all* your needs.
- Faith allows you to experience what you are hoping for.
- God is constantly pouring Jesus' fullness into your soul.
- You are becoming more and more like Jesus.

Here are the key reasons your needs might not be met:

- Jesus is not really your hope.
- You don't understand what is available to you in Him.
- You're going through a season of sin, death, or trauma.
- Something is distracting your faith.
- You're listening to sinful words or thoughts.
- You're struggling with sinful behavior.
- Other people have sinned against you.

In this workbook, we're going to talk about what the fullness of Jesus means for you, particularly where the need for identity is concerned. The last chapter will walk you through practical steps to identify lies, renounce them, and declare God's truth.

I hope the Lord uses this small book to set your heart free from fear, shame, and anything else that might be working to convince you that you are something you are not.

**One key question as you go through this book...**

*Is my heart free to believe what God is saying about who I am?*

# Our Identity in Christ Jesus

## THE NEED OF IDENTITY, PART 1

# CHAPTER 1

# WHO AM I?

*Experiencing the Fullness of Who You Are*

*Therefore, you are no longer a slave, but a son; and if a son, then an heir through God.*
—GALATIANS 4:7

Growing up, I felt like I lived in the shadow of my brother, Bud, who was twelve years older than I was. Not only was he good at everything he did, but he was also loving and caring—a genuinely good person. I didn't get to spend a lot of time with him because he attended college in another state and then went into the military, and he gradually began to seem larger than life to me.

My parents would say, "Why can't you be like Bud?" That felt like an impossible task to me—because Bud was the greatest boy who ever lived! For a teenager who didn't know Jesus, these impossible comparisons pushed me in the other direction. Since I obviously could not be excellent, I became the troublemaker. Where Bud was loving and caring, I was the jerk of the family.

When I was in tenth grade, the school guidance counselor told me I would never amount to anything. I believed her, and I lived my life in line with what I believed. That "identity" pushed my thoughts, my words, and all my actions. I saw myself as a failure in every way except sports. Sports became the only avenue of success for me, or so I thought. If I didn't have sports, the people around me would think I was a failure. That seemed like truth to my heart.

As human beings, we live from our sense of identity—who we *believe* we are. True or false, that sense of identity drives us. Proverbs 23:7 says, "As a man thinks within himself, so he is." What we think and believe about ourselves is what we become. If we believe we are a failure, we will likely become a failure. If we believe we are successful, there is a strong possibility we will be successful. What we believe about ourselves often comes true. Our self-identity determines where we go in life.

One time I was part of a team that was ministering to a young lady dealing with sexual addiction. As we were praying with her, the Lord revealed that the root of her addiction came from being date-raped at the age of sixteen.

When that horrible event occurred, she believed the lie that she was used and dirty, and she began to live out what she believed about herself. Today as I write this, I am so grateful I get to tell you that the Lord healed her heart, and she discovered the truth of her identity. As a result, everything changed. Her life transformed. A new identity—the truth of God—took up residence in her heart, and it dramatically shifted how she lived her life.

## THE SOURCE OF OUR IDENTITY

Whenever we talk about identity, one of the first things we need to address is the source we're using. What *determines* our sense of identity? What source are we relying on to tell us who we are?

The world will try to tell us who we are based on what we do and how we feel, but believers in Jesus have a different source. *God* is the One who tells us who we are. He created us to receive our identity from Him.

The manufacturer of an automobile determines the automobile's identity or name. Outside sources can attempt to re-name or re-identify an automobile, but the true identity is established by its maker. Our God is the One who created us; therefore, He is the only One who has the legal right to determine our true identity.

> Now, thus says the Lord, your Creator, O Jacob,
> And He who formed you, O Israel,
> "Do not fear, for I have redeemed you;
> I have called you by name; you are Mine!"
>
> —ISAIAH 43:1

> Know that the Lord Himself is God;
> It is He who has made us, and not we ourselves;
> We are His people and the sheep of His pasture.
>
> —PSALM 100:3

Others may try to push their opinions of our identity into our heart, but any source for identity other than God is a lie.

One of my favorite books is *You Are Special*, a children's book written by Max Lucado. It's the story of a downtrodden wooden boy in serious need of identity. He discovers that his identity can come only from the one who made him.[1] We are like that wooden toy—our identity can come only from the One who made us. God is the source for our identity.

---

[1] Max Lucado, *You Are Special* (Wheaton, IL: Crossway, 1997).

## THE TWO FACETS OF IDENTITY

A coin has two facets that make up its "identity." The first facet is determined by the image on the coin's front, which is called heads, and the second facet is determined by the image on the back, which is called tails. The combination of both sides determines the coin's identity. We are like a coin in that our identity has two facets: who we are in Jesus and who He is in us. When we understand how this works, we can live with direction, intentionality, confidence, and a fulfillment of destiny.

The first facet—who we are in Jesus—becomes established when we receive Him as our Lord and Savior. We essentially place the totality of our past—who we used to be and what we have done—on the cross and take up the identity of God's only begotten Son.

> More than that, I count all things to be loss in view of the surpassing value of knowing Christ Jesus my Lord, for whom I have suffered the loss of all things, and count them but rubbish so that I may gain Christ, and may be found in Him [this is the first facet of identity], not having a righteousness [a sense of identity] of my own derived from the Law, but that which is through faith in Christ, the righteousness [a sense of identity] which comes from God on the basis of faith.
>
> —PHILIPPIANS 3:8–9

In this context, identity and righteousness are much the same because of Jesus. Our identity does not come from us; it comes from Christ and our position "in Christ." If our identity comes from us, it is not identity at all. It is not real. Our identity—our righteousness—can come only from God.

The second facet of our identity is also deeply, beautifully wrapped up in God. It is *His* identity as He lives inside us.

> I have been crucified with Christ; and it is no longer I who live, but **Christ lives in me**; and the life which I now live in the flesh I live by faith in the Son of God, who loved me and gave Himself up for me.
>
> —GALATIANS 2:20

For the believer in Jesus, the identity of Christ in us is a treasure far greater than anything we could drum up on our own. What we believe about Jesus in us determines what He can do in, through, and around us. That is essentially what Galatians 2:20 means.

Jesus Himself lived from both facets of identity. He revealed His reliance on them when He declared that the Father was in Him (the identity of God inside Him), and He was in the Father (His identity in the Father).

> Do you not believe that **I am in the Father, and the Father is in Me**? The words that I say to you I do not speak on My own initiative, but the Father abiding in Me does His works. "Believe Me that **I am in the Father and the Father is in Me**, otherwise believe because of the works themselves.
>
> —JOHN 14:10–11

# JESUS THE FILLER OF OUR NEEDS | IDENTITY

Jesus used this wording and different variations of it multiple times in the Gospel of John. He was telling the disciples who He really was in John 14, and during this discourse, one of them asked about the Father's reality. Jesus replied that His Father's reality and identity were expressed in Him—in Jesus. His identity also came from being placed "in" the Father.

> That they may all be one; even as You, Father, are in Me and I in You, that **they also may be in Us**, so that the world may believe that You sent Me. . . . **I in them** and You in Me, that they may be perfected in unity, so that the world may know that You sent Me, and loved them, even as You have loved Me.
>
> —JOHN 17:21, 23

You and I are called into the same relationship with God. Everything Paul labored to communicate in the New Testament can be summarized in those two facets of identity.

> To whom God willed to make known what is the riches of the glory of this mystery among the Gentiles, which is **Christ in you**, the hope of glory. We proclaim Him, admonishing every man and teaching every man with all wisdom, so that we may present **every man complete in Christ**. For this purpose also I labor, striving according to His power, which mightily works within me.
>
> —COLOSSIANS 1:27–29

When we walk in the reality of who we really are—Jesus in us and us in Jesus—great things can happen. We become unified the way He intended, and the world comes to know that He loves us.

When we live in the fullness of God's identity for us, we have freedom, life, and confidence. However, when we do *not* live in our God-given identity, we find ourselves getting "needy." Our need for identity goes unmet, which causes us to malfunction from the inside out.

## IN SUMMARY . . .

Our identity "in Jesus" tells us who we are—we are found in the Person of Jesus. Colossians 3:3 says our life (or identity) is "hidden with Christ in God." Being in Christ tells us *who* we are, and Ephesians 2:1–6 tells us *where* we are: seated with Christ in heavenly places. God is a spiritual being, so our identity in the spirit is the most important thing to Him.

The second facet of our identity is the God who dwells inside us. *His* identity establishes our source for life and our ability to live. John declared, "You are from God, little children, and have overcome them; because greater is He who is in you than he who is in the world" (1 John 4:4). We get to live in victory *not* because of who we are as humans—but because of the presence of the One dwelling inside us. His presence inside us is our source of everything and our ability to live a wonderfully victorious life on earth.

The two facets of identity are so big that I have broken them up into two workbooks. This workbook is completely devoted to looking at our identity "in Christ," while the second workbook will look at His identity in us. My goal here is to help people discover their true identity. Not what the world says or what their past says, but what the Bible says. This workbook follows this basic pattern:

1. Are we needy in the area of identity? How can we tell? What are some of the signs?
2. What keeps us from receiving our identity in Jesus? What hinders our faith and tries to keep us from really believing it?
3. How do we respond in faith to what God's Word says and establish our identity in Him?

## TIME TO PRAY

Before we go further, I want to ask you to stop and pray. Then consider this question: "Who am I?" Resist the temptation to say what you think *should* be said, but what does your heart say about who you are? Write down the first thing that comes to your mind.

# CHAPTER 2

# THE IDENTITY OF GOD

*We all, with unveiled face, beholding as in a mirror the glory of the Lord, are being transformed into the same image from glory to glory, just as from the Lord, the Spirit.*

—2 CORINTHIANS 3:18

In the last chapter, I talked about how I used to believe I was a failure. That "identity," which wasn't real but *felt* real to me, pushed me to think, speak, and act according to failure and defeat. But during my junior year of college, my life transformed as I began discovering what God was saying to me—and about me. My identity shifted. It went from "I am a failure" to "I am a man who can do all things through Christ who empowers me."

My heart began to think differently about who I was. Though I began as a person who lived selfishly, indulging himself in the world and what it offered, I became a person who wanted to grow in loving God and other people. When I realized the fullness of God's identity for me, it saved me and changed everything.

The identity of the One who dwells in us is powerful and capable of transforming everything it touches. Our identity "in Christ" is a key part of being transformed into His image (Romans 8:29). All the fullness of God is working to birth in us the identity of Jesus. As we become more like Him, we fulfill our eternal purpose—the reason we exist.

## IDENTITY IN SCRIPTURE

In present-day Christianity, a lot of people talk about identity, even identity in Jesus, so it's kind of surprising to learn that the word *identity* is not in Scripture. It is not present in any English translation. How can we talk so much about identity when the word isn't even in the Bible?

The short answer is, the *concept* of identity completely floods the Word of God. He might not have put the specific word in there, but the concept is there, and it is everywhere. Let's look at how the Bible teaches this topic without actually mentioning it.

## IDENTITY AND GOD'S WORDS

> He humbled you and let you be hungry and fed you with manna which you did not know, nor did your fathers know, that He might make you understand that **man does not live by bread alone, but man lives by everything that proceeds out of the mouth of the Lord**.
>
> —DEUTERONOMY 8:3

God established our identity at the foundation of the world, when He wrote our name in the Lamb's Book of Life. From that moment, we were predestined to become more like Jesus (Revelation 17:8; Romans 8:29).

The process of our true identity taking root in our heart began when we were conceived (Psalm 139:13–18). The problem is, the world is full of sin, and when we were born, we bore the "image of the earthy" (1 Corinthians 15:49).

When Paula and I had kids, we decided in advance not to find out their gender until they were born. The first words spoken in the delivery room were, "It's a boy!" or "It's a girl!" The second key thing spoken over each of our kids was their name. In one form or another, those two declarations are made over every person on the earth. The words declared over us as babies are a foundation of our identity in the physical world.

The core of who we are is established by words. We live on every word that comes from the mouth of God; our identity comes from His voice, and we live on the words He has spoken. Even Jesus' identity was based on His Father's words about Him (Matthew 4:1–4).

Words that form our identity can be verbal or nonverbal. Verbal words are physically or spiritually spoken over us. When God changed Abram's name to *Abraham*, He spoke out loud and gave Abraham the identity of being the father of many nations. Very often when I was young, people spoke negative words to me. Those words affected the course of my life, as well as the manner in which I lived. But then one day the mother of a girl I was dating in high school began to speak words of life over me. She encouraged me instead of tearing me down and helped me believe I could do anything. She played a huge role in my life just with her encouragement. I still remember her all these years later.

Our identity can also be established through nonverbal words expressed through an action or work. Jesus gave the greatest nonverbal word of love and acceptance when He died in our place on the cross, and He gave us another incredible gift when He bestowed on us all the glory His heavenly Father gave Him (John 17:22). The glory Jesus gave us establishes our identity as sons and daughters of the Most High God. Conversely, James wrote about showing preferential treatment to the rich over the poor. Giving preferential treatment to the wealthy communicates a nonverbal message that gives an identity to poor people that is contrary to God's truth.

Our adversary the devil understands that words are the foundation of our identity. From the moment we are conceived, he tries to get people to speak lies over us. I have seen many men with artistic gifting be assaulted and hurt by nonverbal lies. The enemy came along and tried to convince them that there was something wrong with them because they didn't enjoy "guy stuff" like hunting, fishing, or sports. These nonverbal assaults caused many of these men to become confused about their identity and who God called them to be. A man who likes the arts is just as much of a man as one who likes sports. There is no difference.

In summary, the foundation of our identity begins with words. We were created to exist on the words of God. The enemy tries to distract us from those words by giving us *other* words that are lies. These lying words can come from people, from ourselves, even from the devil, but the truth is that we were created for *God's* words. That is where we live.

To understand the biblical perspective of identity, we need to become familiar with the kind of words God is speaking to us. We also need to understand what He wants His words to accomplish in our life.

## GOD'S GLORY AND IDENTITY

> For we did not follow cleverly devised tales when we made known to you the power and coming of our Lord Jesus Christ, but we were eyewitnesses of His majesty. For **when He received honor and glory** from God the Father, such an utterance as this was made to Him by the Majestic Glory, "**This is My beloved Son** with whom I am well-pleased"—and we ourselves heard this utterance made from heaven when we were with Him on the holy mountain.
> —2 PETER 1:16–18

Even though we won't find the English word *identity* in any translations of Scripture, two biblical words correlate to the concept of identity: *image* and *glory*.

The New Testament word for *glory* in Greek literally means "thoughts, opinions, and recognition."[1] How does this relate to identity? We start to get a clue as we look at how *glory* is used in Scripture. For example, while speaking with God the Father on Mount Sinai, Moses asked to see His glory (Exodus 33:18–21).

God replied, "You cannot see My face, for no man can see Me and live!" (verse 20). Most of us are physically known by our faces. If we can see someone's face, we can see their "glory" and therefore identify them. To see God the Father's face is to see His glory, and seeing His glory is seeing His identity.

Another interesting biblical use of the word *glory* is found in 2 Peter 1:16–18, when Peter was describing his experience with Jesus on the Mount of Transfiguration. He wrote that Jesus received "glory" when God the Father declared over Him, "This is My beloved Son with whom I am well-pleased." That simple statement sums up all God's thoughts, opinions, and recognition of Jesus—He is the Father's beloved Son. Those words are an identity statement.

What God the Father declares about *us* is also His glory. What He says about us is who we are in His sight. The Greek word for "glory" (*doxa*) doesn't automatically mean "identity," but it does communicate the idea. Here are two intriguing points about identity and glory in Scripture.

**We were created for God's glory.** When we consider His glory, we need to realize it isn't just a flat plane—something fairly simple and easy to understand—but it is *multifaceted*. First, His glory declares who He is, as we just saw in Moses' story. Second, His glory declares who He created us to be and how He sees us (John 5:44). Finally, God created us to look like Him—to have His likeness. This means everything we think, say, and do can reflect His glory and what *He* is like (1 Corinthians 10:31).

---

[1] Spiros Zodhiates, *The Complete Word Study Dictionary: New Testament*, electronic ed. (Chattanooga, TN: AMG Publishers, 2000).

> Everyone who is called by My name,
> And whom **I have created for My glory**,
> Whom I have formed, even whom I have made.
> —ISAIAH 43:7

> Seeing that His divine power has granted to us everything pertaining to life and godliness, through the true knowledge of Him who **called us by [or to] His own glory** and excellence.
> —2 PETER 1:3

We were created to exist in God's thoughts, opinions, and recognition—who He says we are. In fact, sin is thinking, speaking, or doing something that is *outside* God's thoughts, opinions, and recognition. Sin looks like falling short of His glory (Romans 3:23). God is a spiritual, faith-oriented being. He always sees and operates in faith, and our true identity flows out of the revelation of His glory. If our sense of identity does not flow from His glory, we aren't able to function as who we really are.

We don't pick up a General Motors owner's manual to find out how to operate a Toyota Corolla. We look in the Corolla's manual to learn about the Corolla, because it will tell us the car's identity, function, and purpose. Along the same lines, God's glory is the source of who we are. Not only does His glory define who He is, but it also defines who we are and how we need to see ourselves. We were created to receive His glory with our whole heart and allow it to form our identity.

**We have the glory/identity of Jesus.** What Jesus did for us is just astounding. He has given us *many* wonderful things, and one of His most amazing gifts to us is *His* identity. He gave us the same identity God the Father gave Him.

> The glory which You have given Me I have given to them, that they may be one, just as We are one.
> —JOHN 17:22

Everything God declared over Jesus has been given to us. The glory of Jesus defines who we are. Here are some of the incredible descriptions of His glory in Scripture. All of these things are true about you because of Jesus:

- God the Father called Jesus *beloved* in Matthew 3:17, so we also are called beloved (1 John 3:1–3).
- God the Father called Jesus His Son, and we are also called the sons and daughters of God (Galatians 4:6–7; 2 Corinthians 6:18).
- God the Father said over Jesus, "In whom I am well pleased." When we receive by faith everything God is saying *to* us and the beautiful things He is saying *over* us, we enter into His pleasure (Hebrews 11:6; 10:38). Our Father rejoices over us (Zephaniah 3:17).
- Jesus is the overcomer of the world (John 16:33). We, too, are overcomers of the world (1 John 5:4–5).
- Jesus is the heir of all things (John 3:35; Hebrews 1:2), and we are co-heirs with Him (Romans 8:16–17; Galatians 4:7). What an incredible inheritance!

It is amazing to consider how we have the identity of Jesus. It is a powerful gift, full of love and surrounded by the reservoir of God's grace. One of the most powerful gifts we have is the glory and identity of Jesus. When we receive God's glory for our life, it transforms us into its image (2 Corinthians 3:18). God is not calling us *to try to become* like Jesus; He is calling us to receive by faith the word of His glory, which will transform us into His likeness (1 Thessalonians 2:13; 1 John 3:2–3). When we receive His glory by faith, we take on His identity.

## GOD'S IMAGE AND IDENTITY

> He [Jesus] is the image of the invisible God, the firstborn of all creation.
> —COLOSSIANS 1:15

Another word the Bible uses to communicate the idea of identity is *image*. In Greek the word is *eikon*, which is defined as "to be like, resemble. A representation, an image."[2] Jesus carried the image of Father God, which means He carried the Father's identity. When Philip asked Jesus to show them the Father, Jesus responded pretty strongly because His identity and the Father's identity were the same. Philip had already seen the Father, because he had seen Jesus.

We, too, have the awesome privilege of bearing the image/identity of Jesus. That is our overarching, eternal destiny—to become like Him more and more (2 Corinthians 3:18).

## IN SUMMARY . . .

Identity is not directly mentioned in God's Word, but we can see it again and again. Our identity is clearly a subject important to God the Father's heart. Three foundational ideas communicate our identity in Christ Jesus:

God's Word, which contains His declarations over us

His glory, which is His thoughts, opinions, and recognition of us

The idea of *image,* which is used to communicate likeness and representation.

Those three things—God's Word, His glory, and His image—describe who *you* are. Many people don't have a clue about who they are, yet it is possible to uncover the truth of your identity and have this need finally, beautifully met.

---

[2] Zodhiates, *Word Study Dictionary.*

# CHAPTER 3

# BENEFITS OF OUR IDENTITY IN JESUS

*Bless the LORD, O my soul,*
*And forget none of His benefits.*

—PSALM 103:2

When someone is training for a sport, they expect to see the benefits of their training, and they will use those benefits to monitor their progress. If the benefits are not there, they know they need to change their training.

As we start taking on the fullness of Christ regarding our identity, certain benefits begin to manifest in our life. Here are a few of the benefits we can experience when we are filled with the identity of Jesus.

### KNOWING OUR IDENTITY TRANSFORMS US INTO HIS LIKENESS

*We all, with unveiled face, beholding as in a mirror the glory of the Lord, are being transformed into the same image from glory to glory, just as from the Lord, the Spirit.*

—2 CORINTHIANS 3:18

The primary benefit of saturating ourselves with Jesus' identity is that we start to look like Him. The Christian life is not about being rigid and strict with discipline, nor is it about conforming to rules and laws. Instead, the Christian life is about being transformed into the likeness of Jesus by seeing and receiving God's glory. We were *made* for His glory. The decision to focus on His glory transforms us into the likeness of what we're seeing.

### KNOWING OUR IDENTITY HELPS US REALIZE WE DO NOT LACK

*For in Him all the fullness of Deity dwells in bodily form, and in Him you have been made complete, and He is the head over all rule and authority.*

—COLOSSIANS 2:9–10

I've overheard a lot of people talk about how they lack or just don't have what it takes to overcome an obstacle or accomplish something God has called them to, but God says that "in Christ Jesus" we do not lack. The completeness *Jesus has* is ours. So if we talk about how we lack, we are actually saying that *Jesus* lacks.

When we realize we have no lack because of Jesus, we will become completely confident in His sufficiency. His completeness is our completeness.

## KNOWING OUR IDENTITY EMPOWERS OUR THOUGHTS, WORDS, AND ACTIONS

> For as he thinks within himself, so he is.
> —PROVERBS 23:7

Jesus rebuked the religious leaders of His day for focusing on how a person looked or what a person did. He went on to say that if we want to change someone, we have to change their inside, not their outside. The heart is where the "programming" of our identity is stored, so when our heart is changed, we are changed (Matthew 23:25–26). Whatever exists in our heart forms our programming and determines what we think, say, and do. The way we think is the way we *are*. When our heart's programming is built on our identity in Jesus, we will think, speak, and act out of who we really are: a child of God. What we think, say, and do will look God-like, because He is our Father.

I know a man who was conceived during a one-night stand, and he never knew his dad. He and his mother lived above the bar where his mother worked, and he saw himself as fatherless. He based his identity on his ability to drink and fight—things he learned at the bar—and he struggled with strong self-hatred and anger. But when he was born again, he began to receive a new identity: that of a son of God. I watched his life transform. He went from being a fighter and drinker to being a mature man of God who is a loving husband, father, grandfather, friend, and pastor.

As this precious man experienced, when we receive the spiritual revelation of our identity in Jesus, our life will be transformed into His likeness. "He is like this. Therefore, I am like this."

## KNOWING OUR IDENTITY SETS US FREE TO SERVE

> Jesus, knowing that the Father had given all things into His hands, and that He had come forth from God and was going back to God, got up from supper, and laid aside His garments; and taking a towel, He girded Himself. Then He poured water into the basin, and began to wash the disciples' feet and to wipe them with the towel with which He was girded.
> —JOHN 13:3–5

The character of Jesus looks like service. It doesn't matter how the people gathered around Him respond; He will serve them because serving is what He's like. When we receive the identity of our Savior, we receive His nature and character. We become empowered to do what He does—serving others without having to worry about our own rights or needs.

**JESUS** THE FILLER OF OUR NEEDS | **BENEFITS OF OUR IDENTITY IN JESUS**

Jesus was able to serve this way because He was so confident in His identity in the Father. It didn't matter what others said about Him or what they did to Him.[1] In the same way, when we know our identity in God, we can serve others freely, without any fears of missing out or suffering loss.

## KNOWING OUR IDENTITY HELPS US WALK IN UNITY

> The glory which You have given Me I have given to them, that they may be one, just as We are one.
> —JOHN 17:22

When the focus of our life is God's glory, we experience two major changes.

First, as we've been talking about, His glory transforms us into His likeness, and the likeness of God is love. Second, we are set free from ourselves! Being transformed into the likeness of Jesus releases us from being fixated on our own pleasure, wants, and needs. All our energy doesn't have to go into trying to please ourselves anymore. Instead, we are able to look for opportunities to love others by giving to them and helping them. Living this way—in the truth of who we are—creates an atmosphere of unity.

## KNOWING OUR IDENTITY GIVES US DIRECTION

> Moreover, Shaphan the scribe told the king saying, "Hilkiah the priest has given me a book." And Shaphan read it in the presence of the king. When the king heard the words of the book of the law, he tore his clothes.
> —2 KINGS 22:10–11

What did King Josiah hear in the book of the law that caused him to react so intensely?

He heard about his identity—who he was and what he was meant to focus on. In 2 Kings 22, no one had read God's Word in a long time. Josiah commissioned a priest to restore and clean out the temple, which was when they found a declaration that prophetically mentioned Josiah by name years before he was born (1 Kings 13:2). When Josiah heard his name—*that* is what struck him. The reality of his identity. He suddenly knew the direction and destiny of his kingdom. He knew what to do (2 Kings 23:1–25).

Whenever we hear God's Word and accept into our heart the reality of who we are in Jesus, we will be empowered like Josiah was. That is what happened to me, personally. I went from not knowing my identity and struggling hard to succeed in my relationship with Jesus—to reading His Word and realizing the truth of my identity in Him. As a result, I started living with direction and purpose.

And you can too.

---

[1] Read John 13:2–5; 17:22 for examples.

## KNOWING OUR IDENTITY HELPS US LIVE WITH CONFIDENCE

> Now as they observed the confidence of Peter and John and understood that they were uneducated and untrained men, they were amazed, and began to recognize them as having been with Jesus.
>
> —ACTS 4:13

For me, there is no greater compliment than for someone to look at me and say, "You look like you have been with Jesus." Peter and John walked closely with Jesus for three years, and they took on His identity. The result of saturating themselves with Jesus was an extreme kind of confidence. They spoke like Him. They lived like Him. They acted like Him.

As the disciples experienced, when we saturate ourselves with who Jesus is, His confidence—the confidence of the Son of God—will manifest in our life.

## IN SUMMARY . . .

The benefits of saturating ourselves with Jesus are more than can be counted. When we take on His identity, we are taking on His reality, where there is no lack—ever. *He* empowers our thoughts, words, and actions. *He* empowers our relationships with others and even creates in us a passion to serve others. *He* empowers us to live confidently in His vision and direction for our life. When we take on Jesus' identity, we take on everything He is and everything He does.

# CHAPTER 4

# SYMPTOMS OF THE NEED FOR IDENTITY

We know when our body needs food and water because of the physical symptoms it projects. When we're starving, we can feel it. When we're dehydrated, our body tells us. In the same way, we can know which soulish need is manifesting in our life by looking at its symptoms.

As you read through the following symptoms, allow the Holy Spirit to illuminate any areas in your life where your faith is (currently) unable to fully believe the identity you have in God. One or any combination of the following symptoms can signal a need for identity.

### A NEED FOR IDENTITY CAUSES COMPARISON

> For we are not bold to class or compare ourselves with some of those who commend themselves; but when they measure themselves by themselves and compare themselves with themselves, they are without understanding. But we will not boast beyond our measure, but within the measure of the sphere which God apportioned to us as a measure, to reach even as far as you.
> —2 CORINTHIANS 10:12–13

Comparing ourselves with others is one symptom that can arise when we don't know who we are. If we don't know who we are, our soul will quickly look for an outside source that can give us information regarding our identity. When that source is not God's glory, it can be a person or some type of standard that feels "safe" to us. "I am relying on this standard to tell me who I am. It will let me know how I'm doing compared to others."

A lack of identity can cause us to compare, measure, or classify ourselves with other people or some type of man-made standard. God created you to be *you*, and He wants you to be you, not some imitation of another person or an artificial standard.

Saul, the first king of Israel, did not understand what it meant to be himself. Unfortunately, he had a deep need for identity that went unmet, and his story reveals multiple symptoms of this need. In 1 Samuel 18:8–9, we find a good example of comparison and what can happen when we try to use comparison to tell us who we are:

> Then Saul became very angry, for this saying displeased him; and he said, "They have ascribed to David ten thousands, but to me they have ascribed thousands. Now what more can he have but the kingdom?" Saul looked at David with suspicion from that day on.

Comparing ourselves with others can easily produce three negative emotions:

1. **An "I can't" mentality.** Saul was jealous of David, his successor, and he clearly felt intimidated by him. It was like Saul believed he just wasn't good enough and would never measure up.

2. **Fear.** This negative emotion can cause us to isolate. When we compare, measure, or classify ourselves with others, we can start to see other people as a threat, which produces fear. Saul was afraid of David's popularity with the people.

   This whole process caused the religious leaders of Jesus' day to crucify Him. A lack of identity caused the Pharisees to unhealthily compare themselves with Jesus. The comparison caused them to fear losing their place with the Romans and the people. The fear in turn caused them to want to put Jesus to death. "Therefore the chief priests and the Pharisees convened a council, and were saying, "What are we doing? For this man is performing many signs. **If we let Him go on like this, all men will believe in Him, and the Romans will come and take away both our place and our nation**" (John 11:47–48).

3. **Pride.** A lack of identity can cause us to have a heart of pride. We generate this kind of heart to protect ourselves from the ones we have compared ourselves to. A heart of pride is the opposite of a heart of humility. This is my definition of a heart of humility: one that has a proper perspective of God and others, while depending on God and others.

In Luke 18:9–14, Jesus told a parable about a Pharisee who compared himself with someone he considered a "sinner." He basically said, "Thank You, God, that I'm not like that guy!" Comparing ourselves with another person is never healthy. If it doesn't result in thoughts of defeat, it likely will push us into pride.

## A NEED FOR IDENTITY CAUSES A PEOPLE-PLEASING MINDSET

> The fear of man brings a snare,
> But he who trusts in the Lord will be exalted.
> —PROVERBS 29:25

> How can you believe, when you receive glory from one another and you do not seek the glory that is from the one and only God?
>
> —JOHN 5:44

When we don't know who we are, our soul can easily be tempted to try to please others. We fall into this trap because our soul needs to know who it is, and picking other people as our source seems like a good plan. When we have set other people as our source, we will want to please them to receive their affirmation. People pleasing is a form of slavery to others' standards and desires (Galatians 1:10). We may not *feel* like a slave, but that is how we are living and how we have set up our life.[1]

King Saul was focused on people pleasing. Because he didn't know who he was, he needed people in authority to see him, hear him, and think well of him (1 Samuel 15:24, 30).

### A NEED FOR IDENTITY CAUSES A PERFORMANCE MINDSET

> The tempter came and said to Him, "If You are the Son of God, command that these stones become bread."
>
> —MATTHEW 4:3

This is similar to people pleasing. When we don't know who we are, it is easy to start *performing* for God, ourselves, and others. Performance causes us to focus on what we are doing or not doing instead of who our God says we are.

The temptation to perform was what the devil tried to use against Jesus to get Him to validate who He was as the Son of God.[2] We cannot ever turn enough stones to bread to establish our identity.

We find an example of performance, once again, in Saul's life. He set up a monument for himself in 1 Samuel 15:12. He wanted to make sure that others recognized how "good" he was and remembered him well. As a more modern example, a professional athlete who struggles with performance won't be able to rest after winning a championship. They will immediately have to win the next championship, and then the next, to be satisfied.

### DIFFICULTY SUBMITTING TO AUTHORITY AND AN ATTITUDE OF INDEPENDENCE

> Do you not know that when you present yourselves to someone as slaves for obedience, you are slaves of the one whom you obey, either of sin resulting in death, or of obedience resulting in righteousness?
>
> —ROMANS 6:16

A lack of identity caused King Saul to rebel against God (1 Samuel 13:9–13; 15:13–14). Saul did not receive his identity from the Lord; therefore, when things were tough, submitting to and obeying God wasn't something he could easily do. Whether we are aware of this or not, we end up submitting ourselves to the authority of the thing or person we establish as the source of our identity. This is good when we want to be like Jesus. It is painful when we want to be like someone else or just don't know who we are.

---

[1] The Lord is the One who comforts you. He is with you, and you never need to be afraid of the people around you, even when they seem to be a threat (Isaiah 51:12).
[2] The full story is found in Matthew 3:17–4:11.

When we don't know what God is saying about our identity—but we know we don't want to be people pleasers—we usually turn toward independence and rebellion. Our soul *must* have an identity in order to function, and if there is no external source telling us who we are, we can become independent and self-focused; *we* become the source.

Jesus knew who He was. As a result, He was able to be obedient even to the point of death.

## A NEED FOR IDENTITY CAUSES US TO RECOGNIZE OTHERS ACCORDING TO THE FLESH

> Therefore from now on we recognize no one according to the flesh; even though we have known Christ according to the flesh, yet now we know Him in this way no longer.
> —2 CORINTHIANS 5:16

The flesh is not inherently "wicked." A lot of what the flesh does is just part of everyday life—eating, drinking, sleeping, etc. But the flesh becomes a huge problem when we start relying on it to give us our identity. It cannot be the source that tells us who we are. When we "recognize" someone according to the flesh, this means we aren't looking at them the way Jesus does, but we are basically rating or judging that person according to their physical body, race, human qualifications, performance, abilities, or how they've suffered in life.[3]

## A NEED FOR IDENTITY CAUSES GRASSHOPPER SYNDROME

> So they gave out to the sons of Israel a bad report of the land which they had spied out, saying, "The land through which we have gone, in spying it out, is a land that devours its inhabitants; and all the people whom we saw in it are men of great size. There also we saw the Nephilim (the sons of Anak are part of the Nephilim); and we became like grasshoppers in our own sight, and so we were in their sight." Then all the congregation lifted up their voices and cried, and the people wept that night.
> —NUMBERS 13:32–14:1

Most of the Hebrews God rescued from Egypt were very needy people, and their soulish needs were the main reason they failed to enter their promise. They had massive needs of:

- Identity (Numbers 13:33)
- Security (Numbers 14:3)
- Purpose (Numbers 13:26–31)

When we don't know who we are—or who God is—we are defeated before we even begin. When faced with an obstacle in life, we will see ourselves as a "grasshopper" (small and weak or incompetent) because we are comparing

---

[3] To learn more about seeing people according to the flesh, read Philippians 3:3–6; Galatians 5:24.

ourselves to the obstacle. Every time we see an obstacle, we will say, "There is no way I could conquer that." So we don't even try, and we don't trust God to help us.

## IN SUMMARY . . .

Recognizing when you have an identity need is important. The indicators we discussed in this chapter aren't points of condemnation but amazing opportunities for growth. If one of these indicators stood out in your mind and heart as you read this section, make note of it, talk to the Lord about it, and allow Him to reveal if anything is stealing the fullness of *His* identity already inside you.

# CHAPTER 5

# HOW TO SATISFY THE NEED FOR IDENTITY

> *Put on the new self, which in the likeness of God has been created in righteousness and holiness of the truth.*
> —EPHESIANS 4:24

Practically speaking, *how* do we accept the fullness of Jesus, which enables His identity to fill our soul?

That is the subject of this chapter. Before we start, however, I want to say that nothing I have included here is a formula for "how to receive stuff from God." His fullness is a *Person* named Jesus. What I've written in this chapter will help you position your heart to accept, and live out of, the fullness of identity found in Christ. Think of the following information as a list of suggestions.

## MADE BY GOD AND FOR GOD

> For **by Him all things were created**, both in the heavens and on earth, visible and invisible, whether thrones or dominions or rulers or authorities—**all things have been created through Him and for Him**.
> —COLOSSIANS 1:16

> Know that the Lord Himself is God;
> **It is He who has made us, and not we ourselves**;
> We are His people and the sheep of His pasture.
> —PSALM 100:3

The foundation of discovering who we are, and establishing ourselves in that identity, is the realization that we were made by God and for God. If we think we came about by chance, or that natural selection weeded out the weak people so we could live, our soul will be empty. It might take a while for us to mentally become aware of the emptiness, but our heart will know. Or if we think our identity is something we choose on our own, that it's just up to us, we will also be unfulfilled.

Remember, the car's manufacturer is the only one that can give the car its "identity." That is how we are with the Lord. Because He is the One who made us, He is the only One who can truly establish who we are. When we go to Him to find out who we are, our need for identity is *fully* met—completely, absolutely, in every way.

Knowing that our identity comes from God our Maker, let's draw near to Him to receive the fullness of who we are.

### A NEW CREATION, BORN AGAIN IN OUR HEAVENLY FATHER'S LIKENESS

> Therefore if anyone is in Christ, he is a new creature; the old things passed away; behold, new things have come.
>
> —2 CORINTHIANS 5:17

My son bears a lot of my characteristics because he was born from my seed. When we are born again, we are born from the "seed" of God, which is His Word. We are a new creation. Our spirit bears the very likeness of the God who caused our new birth. As we put on our new spiritual identity in Christ Jesus, we will walk and live as a son or daughter of the Most High God. He is calling all of us to put on the spiritual identity we received from Him.

### WHAT GOD SAYS ABOUT US

> The tempter came and said to Him, "If You are the Son of God, command that these stones become bread." But He answered and said, "It is written, 'Man shall not live on bread alone, but **on every word that proceeds out of the mouth of God.**'"
>
> —MATTHEW 4:3–4

We *need* the words of God. He is our heavenly Father, and because He is a loving Father, He wants us to hear His affectionate and passionate declarations about who we are. Our Father is the only One who truly knows who we are; therefore, we can push aside every other source and listen only to His words about our identity.

The words that come out of His mouth establish our true identity, while negative words from people—including ourselves—can give us a "dark" identity, something that brings a form of death into our life. The truth of God's glory satisfies our heart's need to know who we are.

Jesus intentionally received His identity from what His Father said about Him.

> For when He received honor and glory from God the Father, such an utterance as this was made to Him by the Majestic Glory, "This is My beloved Son with whom I am well-pleased."
>
> —2 PETER 1:17

Jesus had no identity other than what His heavenly Father spoke over Him. When the enemy tried to get Jesus to question His identity, Jesus knew exactly who His source was. All that mattered was what the Father said.

The words of God hold transforming power (1 Thessalonians 2:13). When He speaks His glory and truth over us, these things come and fill our soul. The words of God continually work to draw us to Him, like a powerful magnet. His words will not completely return to Him until they have drawn us into their likeness (Isaiah 55:10–11).

To live in the fullness of our identity in Jesus, we have a choice to make—we need to choose to see and hear what God is saying about us. If we do not resolve in our heart that *God* is our source of identity, the world and its many voices will start to overwhelm us. If we give in, we will adopt whatever identity the world wants us to have.

## RECEIVING HIS DECLARATIONS BY FAITH

For whatever is born of God overcomes the world; and **this is the victory that has overcome the world—our faith**.

—1 JOHN 5:4

Just about everything our loving heavenly Father says about us will seem too good to be true. Remember, He is a spiritual being, living and operating in the eternal spiritual realm. The only way to operate in the spiritual is to live by faith, so we need to receive His words about us with a heart of faith. We also need to resist the temptation to hear His declarations and try to perform them. That isn't how it works. He spoke His Word into our life to change us, not for us to try and perform it. *His Word* does the transforming work we need, but for it to do His transforming work, we need to receive His declarations by faith (Hebrews 4:2; 11:6). Once we receive His declarations by faith, they will manifest in the physical realm.

Our God constantly speaks His words and glory over us, which establish who we are. If we have a deep need for identity, then we have a need for what God is saying about us. It isn't that He has stopped speaking, but the need is manifesting because we haven't completely *accepted* what He is saying. The glorious revelations that transform our life will "work" only when we receive them by faith (Hebrews 4:2).

Faith is the assurance of things we're hoping for and the evidence of things we cannot see with our physical eyes. This means that in the beginning, we will not be able to see what we are believing by faith. Faith means not being able to see it—but *knowing* in our heart that it exists or it is coming. When we have received in faith His provisions for us and what He's saying about us, only then will they begin to manifest in our life in the physical. First faith, then sight. The things of God must always begin in the unseen journey of faith.

All our soulish needs are met through faith in Jesus and His sufficiency. Our faith is the key we need to open the door into our identity. God's Word describes what happens when we believe in Jesus: Our nature changes, and we become children of God who can overcome the way He overcomes (1 John 5:4–5). We release His nature into our life through our faith. Verse 4 says, "This is the victory that has overcome the world, even our faith." So, as we receive by faith what God has said over us, we begin to live in our identity in Christ.

## THE HIDDENNESS OF IDENTITY

> Therefore if you have been raised up with Christ, keep seeking the things above, where Christ is, seated at the right hand of God. Set your mind on the things above, not on the things that are on earth. **For you have died and your life is hidden with Christ in God**.
> —COLOSSIANS 3:1–3

I love walking outside on a clear, cloudless night when the moon is full and shines silvery light on everything around me. Sometimes the moon is so bright that the night actually seems full of light, almost like day. The moon itself cannot give light. The moon shines only when it has taken on the characteristics and identity of the sun.

We are like the moon in that we take on the "light" of Jesus' identity as we see and reflect Him. Colossians 3 says we have spiritually died and been hidden in the Person of Jesus. All that He is we have become, because we are inside Him. The more we see Him, the more we take on His identity and reflect Him.

*Seeing* happens with the heart. Not only do we see the Lord with our heart,[1] but the heart is also how others see us. Whatever we project with our heart is our identity. When Jesus is our source, our heart projects Him, which means that others can look at us and see *His* light, not just a human light. But when our source is the world, and we long to be seen by others, praised, and noticed by the world, *that* becomes our identity. The key here is to see ourselves inside Jesus. By the inspiration of the Holy Spirit, Paul wrote that we died "in Christ Jesus." A dead person cannot project an identity anymore. The life we now have is hidden with Christ in God.

When we were baptized, we entered into Jesus' death and burial. A person who has physically died and been buried cannot be seen anymore. If they do happen to be seen, it is not a pretty picture! Similarly, when we project ourselves for others to see, we are giving them a picture that is unbecoming and unattractive.

> Therefore, we have been buried with Him through baptism into death, so that as Christ was raised from the dead through the glory of the Father, so we too might walk in newness of life.
> —ROMANS 6:4

Through baptism, we died and were buried so we could come forth in the "newness of life." This newness is found only in the Person and identity of Jesus. The programming of our heart needs to be rewritten so His spiritual reality becomes our spiritual reality. That's the goal. When our heart is filled with the desire to project or manifest ourselves, instead of Jesus, this is a sign that our identity is established in ourselves. "I am the king here." But when our heart is filled with a passion to project Jesus, *He* is our identity. Our decision to pursue Jesus with all our heart causes our identity to be established in Him. We are hidden in who He is, and His identity shines clearly.

---

[1] We need to be "pure" in heart to see Him. The heart is definitely involved (Matthew 5:8).

## IN SUMMARY . . .

God made us. Therefore, He is the only One who can rightfully establish our identity, which He does by declaring His glory and truth over us. Our part is to receive by faith His glory and truth found "in Christ Jesus." We solidify His identity within us by "hiding" ourselves in His reality.

# CHAPTER 6

# OBSTACLES TO ACCEPTING OUR IDENTITY IN JESUS

*Therefore, since we have so great a cloud of witnesses surrounding us, let us also lay aside every encumbrance and the sin which so easily entangles us, and let us run with endurance the race that is set before us, fixing our eyes on Jesus, the author and perfecter of faith.*

—HEBREWS 12:1–2

The completeness of our identity in Jesus is released through faith. The devil has a whole lot of ways he tries to distract our faith and keep us from focusing on God and the riches of His identity for us. Here are a number of common situations that can keep us from receiving who we are in Jesus.

## A LACK OF KNOWLEDGE ABOUT WHO GOD SAYS WE ARE

My people are destroyed for lack of knowledge.
Because you have rejected knowledge,
I also will reject you from being My priest.
Since you have forgotten the law of your God,
I also will forget your children.
—HOSEA 4:6

Therefore My people go into exile for their lack of knowledge;
And their honorable men are famished,
And their multitude is parched with thirst.
—ISAIAH 5:13

It is virtually impossible to believe something we don't know about. If we haven't heard the information, if no one has explained it to us, and we haven't read it or seen it and have no idea it exists—we can't believe it. That is why one of the enemy's major schemes is to separate us from the revelation of God—the truth about Him, which He wants to share with us. Isaiah 5:13 says we are destroyed or taken captive because of a lack of knowledge.

When we just don't know our identity in Jesus, we can fall prey to all kinds of demonic schemes. Another common scheme is looking for our identity through human, fleshly means (2 Corinthians 5:16). This can look like a bunch of things, but one example is a young man who doesn't understand that God says he is a success, and so he sets out to *prove* he is successful to himself and to others.

Another demonic scheme is getting us to compare ourselves with others and rely on human (not godly) standards (2 Corinthians 10:12–13). For example, a young woman doesn't know or understand that God says she is altogether lovely and there is no blemish in her. As a result, she compares herself with the "beauty" she sees on social media and subsequently feels worthless.

## RELIGIOUS TRADITIONS ABOUT WHO WE ARE

> See to it that no one takes you captive through philosophy and empty deception, according to the tradition of men, according to the elementary principles of the world, rather than according to Christ.
> —COLOSSIANS 2:8

> You no longer permit him to do anything for his father or his mother; thus invalidating the word of God by your tradition which you have handed down; and you do many things such as that.
> —MARK 7:12–13

One of the most powerful weapons in the devil's arsenal is the traditions of men. When a human tradition is planted deep in our heart, it can make even the Word of God ineffective in our life. I have seen *powerful* words from God become ineffective in people's lives because those words didn't line up with their traditions. Human traditions hindered the religious leaders of Jesus' day. Their traditions were powerful enough to keep them from recognizing who Jesus really was and accepting Him by faith. Bill Johnson of Bethel Church in Redding, California, says, "I cannot afford to have a thought in my head about me that is not in His." So very true.

As a modern example of how human traditions can influence us, one "popular" religious tradition says we are sinners saved by grace. One of the problems with this tradition is that it doesn't line up with the truth of God's Word, which calls us *saints* (holy ones). Notice what Paul calls the believers in Rome: "To all who are beloved of God in Rome, called as **saints**" (Romans 1:7). Sixty-one times in the New Testament, believers in Christ Jesus are referred to as saints. The idea that we are "sinners saved by grace" causes a sinful, defeated mindset. Proverbs 23:7 says that we will be whatever we think. If we think we are sinners, it will be much easier for us to sin. I do not like it whenever somebody tries to say, "Well, I'm just a sinner saved by grace." No. You are a man or woman of God who has been set completely free from darkness and given a new nature. You need to believe who God says you are.

## VERBAL CURSES

> Death and life are in the power of the tongue,
> And those who love it will eat its fruit.
> —PROVERBS 18:21

Words contain the power of life and death. We can speak life, or we can speak death. The people around us can speak life, or they can speak death. When someone talks to us, and we receive the power contained in their words, we will begin to walk in the "likeness" of those words. This is an amazing thing when the words are life and look like Jesus, but when the words are contrary to God's truth, we can end up accepting a curse that will bring a form of death into our being.[1] Words—ours or someone else's—can separate us from our identity in Jesus. An unfortunately common example is a young lady who is told she is stupid, no good, or a mistake. If she believes what the other person says, this "curse" will work to divide her from the truth of Jesus.

If you are in a position of authority in someone's life, keep in mind that you have the opportunity to empower their identity in Jesus by what you speak to them.

"You are chosen by God."

"You are flawless in His sight."

"You are not shameful to Him."

"You are the way God created men to be."

"You are the way God created women to be."

## BELIEVING OTHER PEOPLE'S OPINIONS

> How can you believe, when you receive glory from one another and you do not seek the glory that is from the one and only God?
> —JOHN 5:44

Just as a gasoline engine is made to run on gas, we were created to live on God's glory (Isaiah 43:7). Remember, the Greek word for "glory" can be defined as *His* thoughts, *His* opinions, and *His* recognition. We were made for the thoughts and opinions of God—what He says about us, how He thinks about us, how He sees or recognizes us. When we feed our heart His thoughts, opinions, and recognition, we will live in ways we never dreamed possible (but He always dreamed possible). However, if we begin to feed our heart and mind the thoughts, opinions, and recognition of *people*, we will malfunction. Their "glory" will cut off our faith. It's like putting water in a gas tank—it shuts down the engine.

---

[1] The enemy's nature is quite unpleasant (John 8:44).

A sin of *omission* is when a parent or someone in authority fails to do what the person in their care needs from them. When a parent does not speak words of identity and blessing into their child, it is a sin of omission. That child will be very open to believing others' opinions about who they are, because their parent never told them. Think of a young man who never heard words of love and affirmation from his father. He will try to find those words from someone else, and the results will likely be painful.

A sin of *commission* is when a parent or someone in authority speaks words that don't communicate God's truth about the person. These "words" aren't always verbal; they can also be tone of voice, body language, etc. Many children are told there's something "wrong" with them because they don't like what their gender typically likes; that is a sin of commission.

Down through the years, many young men have told me they felt there was something wrong with them because they liked the arts rather than sports. The thoughts and opinions others projected on them caused them to be confused about how God made them. Conversely, I have heard numerous young women talk about how people made them think there was something wrong with them because they liked to do "guy things," like playing football or hunting and fishing.

The thoughts and opinions of people can be a major stumbling block that keeps us from receiving our God-given identity by faith.

## TRAUMATIC EVENTS

> This Moses whom they disowned, saying, "Who made you a ruler and a judge?" is the one whom God sent to be both a ruler and a deliverer with the help of the angel who appeared to him in the thorn bush.
>
> —ACTS 7:35

Moses suffered rejection when he tried to be Israel's deliverer. That traumatic event affected him so deeply that he ran away and spent forty years in the wilderness. He lost his confidence and even developed a speech problem. He could not receive what God was saying over him.

Sometimes traumatic events wound the heart and make it difficult for us to receive God's truth at a deep level. An example of this is a woman who was sexually assaulted as a little girl and came to believe she was dirty and "used." That lie became her identity, making it difficult for her to believe what the Lord was saying. But praise God—He healed her heart and set her free from the lie holding her captive.

## VIEWING OURSELVES ACCORDING TO THE FLESH

> That which is **born of the flesh is flesh**, and that which is born of the Spirit is spirit.
>
> —JOHN 3:6

Before leaving their ship and stepping out into space, an astronaut puts on a space suit. In the same way, before we were born, we put on an "earth suit" called the flesh. Jesus did the same (John 1:14). The flesh is something all of us need in order to be alive, but if our identity comes from the flesh, we will not be able to "see" or accept our spiritual identity in Jesus.

There are three basic problems with the flesh:

- It is tainted with sin (Romans 8:3).
- It is connected to the world, which is under the devil's authority (Ephesians 2:1–3; 2 Corinthians 4:4). The devil constantly tries to enslave us to the world through our flesh.
- The flesh wants to be in charge, and it tries to control us through its appetites, desires, and what the world wants (1 Peter 2:11).

The devil uses all three of these problems to con us into accepting an identity that looks like the flesh, not like Jesus. He wants us to identify ourselves by our physical body, race, qualifications, abilities, performance, and how we've suffered in life.[2] Most of these expressions are not evil in and of themselves, but we were created to see ourselves according to God's glory—everything *He* is saying about us. When our mind is "set on the flesh," bad things happen (Romans 8:6). Namely, we separate ourselves from the spiritual identity that is ours in Jesus.

## BEING SEEN

> Therefore, if you have been raised up with Christ, keep seeking the things above, where Christ is, seated at the right hand of God. Set your mind on the things above, not on the things that are on earth. **For you have died and your life is hidden with Christ in God.**
> —COLOSSIANS 3:1–3

Earlier in this book, we talked about our life being hidden in Jesus. The goal is to reflect Him in everything we do. It is possible for people to look at us and actually see Him. That is what "being hidden" in Him means. The more Jesus is seen and reflected in our heart, the more His identity has become our identity.

When our need for identity is not met, we will do everything we can to meet it. One typical way we try to meet this need is by seeking attention from other people. Setting our heart to be seen is a major hindrance to adopting the identity of Jesus. We cannot have our identity and Jesus' identity at the same time. It would be like the moon telling the sun that it doesn't want to reflect its light anymore. "Thanks, but I'm just going to shine by myself now." The moon has no light of its own. When it separates from sunlight, it grows dark and can project only darkness; darkness becomes its identity when the sun is not involved.

When we set our heart on being seen by others, we are probably projecting ourselves and not Jesus. Obviously, being "famous," having a following, being on TV, being seen by others—these things are not inherently bad, but

---

[2] It doesn't do any good to recognize someone "according to the flesh" (2 Corinthians 5:16).

they can't be the desire of our heart. There is a big difference between Jesus making us famous so others can see *Him* and our efforts to be known and seen on our own, because we don't know who we are in Him.

## IN SUMMARY . . .

As believers in Jesus, we have the amazing opportunity to receive and reflect His identity the same way the moon receives and reflects the sun. When we live in the beauty of this divine reflection, our life becomes gloriously fruitful. We become nearly unstoppable—which is a major problem for the enemy. He will do everything he can to keep us from growing up in Christ and taking on Jesus' identity.

We step into who we are in Jesus through faith. It doesn't happen by works, performance, or anything other than the simplicity of faith. The devil has a whole lot of ways he tries to distract our faith, but the more we are able to keep our eyes on God and His riches of identity, the more we will shine the light of Jesus.

# CHAPTER 7

# THE FULLNESS OF IDENTITY

*Because you are sons, God has sent forth the Spirit of His Son into our hearts, crying, "Abba! Father!" Therefore you are no longer a slave, but a son; and if a son, then an heir through God.*
—GALATIANS 4:6–7

What does God have to say about us as His children? What does He say about how He made us?

When we know what *He* is saying, we can dismiss whatever the world or the enemy is saying. Those voices suddenly become much less important in our life. Knowing the words of God gives us the opportunity to speak what He is speaking, which is the principle of confession. *Confession* means "to speak the same thing," so when we confess or speak out God's truth, we're speaking what He is speaking.

Confessing God's truth is like getting on an elevator and pressing the button for the floor we want. If we don't press a button (confess nothing), the elevator won't move. If we press the button for the floor we're on (confess only our present circumstances), the elevator still won't move. Confession allows us to "push the right button" so we can move with God. In this chapter, we will look at some of the amazing things God is saying about us as His kids.

When we receive Jesus as our Savior, we are established "in Christ," which gives us our position as children of God. God Himself says He is our Father, and we are His sons and daughters:

> "Therefore, come out from their midst and be separate," says the Lord.
> "And do not touch what is unclean;
> And I will welcome you.
> And I will be a father to you,
> And you shall be sons and daughters to Me,"
> Says the Lord Almighty.
> —2 CORINTHIANS 6:17–18

> As many as received Him, to them He gave the right to become children of God, even to those who believe in His name.
> —JOHN 1:12

We are the children of God and He *longs* for us. We are not unwanted, nor are we an inconvenience. The small phrase "in Christ" describes what God did for us following our salvation; He placed us "in" the Person of Jesus. So now, spiritually speaking, whatever happened to Jesus happened to us.

He died. We died.

He was buried. We were buried.

He was raised from the dead. We were raised from the dead.

He sat down next to the Father. We, too, were placed with the Father.

As the children of God, we have a position in the heavenlies with Christ:

> God, being rich in mercy, because of His great love with which He loved us, even when we were dead in our transgressions, made us alive together with Christ (by grace you have been saved), and raised us up with Him, and seated us with Him in the heavenly places in Christ Jesus.
> —EPHESIANS 2:4–6

When we believe in Jesus, we are spiritually placed inside Him and "sealed" there with the Holy Spirit:

> In Him, you also, after listening to the message of truth, the gospel of your salvation—having also believed, you were sealed in Him with the Holy Spirit of promise.
> —EPHESIANS 1:13

Here are a few descriptions of what it means to be "inside" of Jesus:

"In Christ" means we are sons and daughters of God.

- We have a promise from God that we are His children, and we begin walking in that promise when we receive Jesus as our Lord (2 Corinthians 6:18; John 1:12).
- Our spirit carries a heavenly declaration that we are His children (Romans 8:16).
- We are no longer slaves (Galatians 4:7).
- We *desire* our heavenly Father (Galatians 4:6).
- We are God's beloved (1 John 3:1–2).

"In Christ" means we have a place with God.

- We have a place in the Father's house; we aren't merely guests there (John 14:1–3).
- God is our Father and we are His children (Matthew 6:32; 1 John 3:1–2).

- We are seated in the heavenlies and have a rightful place there (Ephesians 2:6–7; Colossians 3:1–3).
- We are born from above; our home is Heaven (John 3:3; John 13:3).
- In Christ we are a new creation (2 Corinthians 5:17).
- We now have *His* nature, which overcomes the world (1 John 5:4–5).
- We are dead to sin but alive to God (Romans 6:11).

"In Christ" means we have everything we need to overcome the powers of darkness.
- Our place is far above all the authorities of darkness (Ephesians 1:17–23).
- God will soon crush the devil under our feet (Romans 16:19–20).
- The One who is in us is greater than any obstacle (1 John 4:4).
- The enemy cannot separate us from God's love (Romans 8:35–39).
- The devil *flees* when we resist him and submit to God (James 4:7).

"In Christ" means we have physical resources.
- He became poor so we could become rich (2 Corinthians 8:9).
- As God's sons and daughters, we are His heirs (Galatians 4:7).
- He supplies all our needs (Philippians 4:19).
- He wants us to bring Him all our requests (John 14:12–14; James 4:2–3).

"In Christ" means we have all the spiritual resources we need to walk in victory.
- We are blessed with every spiritual blessing (Ephesians 1:3).
- God has already given us everything pertaining to life and godliness (2 Peter 1:3).
- Through God's promises we can participate in His nature (2 Peter 1:4).
- Christ lives in and through us (Galatians 2:20). One of the most powerful resources we receive when we are born again is the Spirit of Jesus, who comes and indwells every believer. The Holy Spirit reveals to us the great things God the Father has given us through Jesus, and the Spirit also empowers us to fulfill our destiny as God's children.
- In Christ we are complete and do not lack (Colossians 2:10).

"In Christ" means we have great potential to grow spiritually.
- We are His workmanship (Ephesians 2:10).
- He will finish the work He is doing in us (Philippians 1:6).
- He is faithful to the task (1 Thessalonians 5:24).
- He is working inside us, and we respond by intentionally living out what He is doing (Philippians 2:12–3).

"In Christ" means we have the option of adopting His characteristics.

- We are sanctified. The work is done and finished; we have been *established* as God's children (1 Corinthians 1:2; 6:11; Hebrews 10:10).
- We are perfected by Jesus' work on the cross (Hebrews 10:14).
- We are made holy by Jesus' work on the cross. *Holy* means set apart, uncommon, and clean. Since we are holy in His sight, we are saints (literally "holy ones") of God (Hebrews 10:10; 13:12; 1 Corinthians 1:2).
- Jesus took our sin and gave us His righteousness (2 Corinthians 5:21; 1 Corinthians 1:30).
- We overcome the world's obstacles like He does (1 John 5:4–5).
- We take on His mind (1 Corinthians 2:16).
- We are successful and always headed toward triumph (2 Corinthians 2:14; Romans 8:28).
- We have a place/position with Christ at God's right hand (Ephesians 2:4–6; Colossians 3:1–3).
- We have the capacity to love the way Jesus loves (1 John 4:7–8; 4:19–5:2).

"In Christ" means our past sins and failures are completely forgiven and washed away.

- We have forgiveness in Jesus (1 John 1:9; Hebrews 10:17). Our sins are cast as far as the east is from the west (Psalm 103:12). We need to agree with God and forgive ourselves (Acts 10:15).
- In Christ we can be fully, perfectly cleansed. We are pure, having been cleansed by the blood of Jesus (1 John 1:7–9; Isaiah 1:18).
- In Christ our sins can be forgotten (Hebrews 10:17). Our past is in Jesus' tomb; it is buried, and now we are holy. We need to see ourselves as forgiven, the way He sees us (Romans 6:3–7; Acts 10:15).
- God's ability to redeem the past is far greater than our ability to "blow it" (Romans 5:20).
- We are victorious (2 Corinthians 2:14).

"In Christ" means we are guaranteed a glorious eternal future.

- Jesus will soon return and take us to be with Him (1 Thessalonians 4:16–18).
- We will inherit the world (Romans 4:13).
- We will judge the world (1 Corinthians 6:2).
- We will judge angels (1 Corinthians 6:3).
- We will fully see and experience the glories of God's grace for eternity (Ephesians 2:7).
- We will be with God, face to face, for eternity (Revelation 21:3–4).

Which of those passages is the Holy Spirit highlighting to you?

Begin to confess and declare those Scriptures into your life. A confession (also called a declaration) could sound something like this: "Heavenly Father, by faith I confess that by Your grace I am the beloved of God, like 1 John 3:1–3 says." The full salvation of God is released into our life through the power of our confessions (Romans 10:10).

We are the children of God, and the treasure He has assigned to us is *abundant* and truly awesome. When we focus on and confess His truth, our heart will start to take on His thoughts and opinions. This is definitely a step of faith—because when we start looking at His glory, we will notice how different aspects of our life don't agree with what He is saying about us. But as we see and receive His glory by faith, that same glory will transform our life into His image (2 Corinthians 3:18).

When your heavenly Father reveals a truth to you, respond by continually confessing the truth He revealed, for it is where you are going.

# CHAPTER 8

# WORKING IT OUT

*Reestablishing Your Identity in Jesus*

> *So then, my beloved, just as you have always obeyed, not as in my presence only, but now much more in my absence, work out your salvation with fear and trembling; for it is God who is at work in you, both to will and to work for His good pleasure.*
>
> —PHILIPPIANS 2:12–13

God is doing a good work, and He invites us to participate with Him. His part is setting up His identity inside us; He does the hard work. Our part is to *bring out* what He's doing—to let it be visible in our life. We pay attention to His work and say "yes" to it.

We don't need to make following God more complicated than it is. To participate with Him, we just "bring forth" the incredible things He is doing within us. Where the need for identity is concerned, we receive by faith *His* identity, and we let go of anything that's trying to keep our heart from believing what He is saying over us.

In this chapter, you will have the opportunity to take a practical look at your life and see if you can identify any identity obstacles that you might be struggling with. Very often a lack of identity comes from believing a lie about who you are. Hopefully when you are finished going through this chapter, you will be able to see the lie and where it came from, repent for believing it, and receive God's truth in its place.

Sometimes the greatest challenge we have as believers is simply agreeing with God. I want to remind you of this quote from Bill Johnson: that we cannot afford to have any thoughts regarding our identity that are not God's thoughts.[1] As we begin to agree with God and believe what He is thinking and saying about who we are, we start to live out our *real* identity—who we are in Jesus.

Read the following prayer out loud, from your heart. As you read, pay attention to your feelings and the thoughts that pop up in your conscious mind. Remember, God's Word says He thinks about us the same thoughts He thinks about Jesus (John 17:22). His description of Jesus is His description of *you*.

---

[1] For too often, we go after human opinions instead of the amazing, completely true opinions of Father God (John 5:44).

Lord, thank You that when I received Jesus Christ as my Lord and Savior, You gave me the authority to become Your child. As a child of God, I have a destiny to grow into the likeness of Jesus and express His likeness wherever I go. God has a good plan for my life, and that plan is filled with good works, leading to an eternal life of rewards and blessings. I am Your beloved son/daughter in whom You are well pleased. You declare that I am awesomely and wonderfully made, being altogether beautiful, and there is no blemish in me. When I received You as my Savior, I received Your forgiveness for my sins. You *have* forgiven me. You have cleansed me from the dirtiness of my sins and washed my past. You even chose to forget my past. Through the work and sacrifice of Jesus on the cross, I am perfect. By His precious blood, I am holy and a sanctified saint of God, completely blameless. By the power of Your grace, I am an overcomer. The world's obstacles cannot stop me. I am perfect and complete, lacking in nothing. My identity in Christ is that of a victor. I am rich, blessed, and beloved of God. I confess that You, my Lord and my God, will lead me and abundantly empower me to enter Your eternal kingdom.[2]

How did you feel as you read that prayer? Do you believe the prayer is true for you?

If any parts of that prayer were *difficult* for you to confess out loud and believe, ask the Lord to help you identify why. Every belief in your heart has an origin. *Why* do you believe what you believe about yourself? Where did you hear the *opposite* of what God is saying?

The rest of this chapter will help you identify lies you have believed concerning your identity, as well as where the lies came from. Maybe a traumatic event pressed a lie into your heart. Maybe you suffered a grievous loss or disappointment, or maybe you had a painful encounter with an authority figure that injured your heart. Once you have identified a lie, forgive the person who led you to believe that lie, and ask the Lord to forgive you for believing it. Finally, ask Him to reveal the truth that corresponds to the lie. The removal of the lie doesn't set a person free—knowing the truth sets them free.[3]

## REESTABLISHING YOUR IDENTITY IN JESUS

This section is meant to help you walk in the freedom that is already yours in Jesus. Ask Him to reveal any lies you have believed about your identity, and then ask Him to replace those lies with His Word, which is His truth. His truth, as you accept it and believe it, will set you free every single time.[4]

Here are a few reminders of how God speaks to us. He sent His Holy Spirit to dwell inside the people who believe in Jesus. Most of the time when God speaks to us, He speaks *in* us—in our heart and mind (Matthew 10:20; Hebrews 8:10). Because that's true, His voice often sounds like a thought. But that's where the challenge comes in. We have to learn to discern the origin of our thoughts—whether they are coming from us, from the enemy, or from God.

---

[2] This prayer is based on John 1:12; Mark 1:11; Song of Solomon 4:7; 1 John 1:9; 5:4; Hebrews 10:10–17; Acts 10:15; Ephesians 1:3–4; James 1:4; Colossians 2:10; 2 Corinthians 2:14; 2 Peter 1:11.
[3] For example, if you believe you are nothing but a sinner, the corresponding truth to that lie is that you are a saint in Christ Jesus. If you believe you are powerless, the corresponding truth from Scripture is that you are more than a conqueror in Jesus.
[4] If you have trouble consistently believing what the Bible says, you likely need to renew your mind like Romans 12:2 talks about. Check out my book called *Renewing Your Mind* for more information on this topic.

**JESUS** THE FILLER OF OUR NEEDS | **WORKING IT OUT**

Both the mind and heart generate thoughts. These thoughts often use the pronouns *me* and *I*, because they are us thinking about ourselves. The forces of darkness also can generate thoughts inside us. They will try to plant lies, accusations, and deceptions in our heart and mind (Acts 5:3).

When God speaks, His voice doesn't sound the way the darkness sounds. His voice and what He says will always be in line with the truth of His Word (John 6:63). His voice will manifest the fruit of the Holy Spirit, who is the Spirit of truth (John 16:13). When God speaks to believers in Jesus, He will speak righteousness—that which is *right* about us (John 16:8–10). He actually does not tell us what is *wrong* with us, but He will tell us what is right in Christ Jesus and allow that revelation to reveal anything that isn't right in our thinking or behavior. (That is what happened with the prophet Isaiah in Isaiah 6:1–8).

God loves His kids. He does not pick us apart with critical words, but He genuinely is the God of truth and love. He knocks on the door of our heart, asking to come inside and take up residence in the areas of our heart where we are closed off to Him and His lordship.[5] He will not force His glory into an area where we are closed to Him. (These closed-off places happen when we are clinging to our own will or some type of sin). When Jesus is allowed to take up residence in a new area of our heart, the fullness of the fruit of the Spirit (love, joy, peace, etc.) will manifest in that area. He is coming to be Lord in our life, and the fruit of His lordship will be released through us (Romans 14:16–17).

When He reveals His truth to you, *treasure it*. Hold on to His words, and make them a part of your heart. Remember, we were created for an identity originating from God. Any other type of identity is a false identity that will lead to forms of death.

Consider the following concepts and questions as honestly as you can. Don't let the enemy tell you anything that is untrue, make you feel ashamed, or push you to respond as a victim. Just listen for God's voice, and write down what you discern He tells you.

## 1. A FALSE IDENTITY ORIGINATING FROM SINS OF OMISSION OR COMMISSION

Start off by praying this prayer: "Father God, I acknowledge that I was made to find my identity in Jesus. Would You please show me one area in my life where I have not yet received by faith Your glory and truth about who I am?"

What does He show you? Write it below.

_____
_____
_____
_____

---

[5] The Bible talks about this in Revelation 3:20; Ephesians 3:14–17; 1 Peter 3:15.

## JESUS THE FILLER OF OUR NEEDS | IDENTITY

Does He remind you of a past event? Who was involved in this event? Write your answers below.

_____

_____

_____

_____

Was a sin of *omission* involved in this event? A sin of omission is when the words of affirmation and blessing you needed from your parents and authorities during your formative years were not given to you. Write down your thoughts.

_____

_____

_____

_____

What lie did you start to believe because of this sin of omission?

_____

_____

_____

_____

Was a sin of *commission* involved in this event? This is where a parent or authority figure committed a sin against you. Write down your thoughts.

_____

_____

_____

_____

## JESUS THE FILLER OF OUR NEEDS | WORKING IT OUT

What lie did you start to believe because of this sin of commission? Write it below.

_____

_____

_____

_____

"I forgive these authorities who sinned against me." Write their names below.

_____

_____

_____

_____

"I repent for the following unrighteous responses that I entertained because of their offenses . . ." Write them below.

_____

_____

_____

_____

"I confess God's glory and truth about me. This is what I believe God is saying to me right now." Write it below.

_____

_____

_____

_____

_____

## 2. A FALSE IDENTITY ORIGINATING FROM COMPARING YOURSELF WITH OTHERS

Start off by praying this prayer: "Father God, You made me to find my identity in Jesus, not by comparing myself to others. Have I relied on comparison to tell me who I am? Have I looked to other people or to un-Christlike standards instead of to You as I searched for my identity?"

What does He show you? Write it below.

_____
_____
_____
_____
_____

Does He remind you of a past event? Who was involved in this event? Write your answers below.

_____
_____
_____
_____
_____

What lie did you believe because of this comparison?

_____
_____
_____
_____
_____
_____

"Father God, I forgive the following people . . ."

___

"Lord, I repent for these unrighteous responses . . ."

___

"I renounce this lie . . ."

___

"I declare God's truth . . ."

## 3. A FALSE IDENTITY ORIGINATING FROM IDENTIFYING YOURSELF ACCORDING TO THE FLESH

Start off by praying this prayer: "Father God, I acknowledge that my identity is found in You and in *Your* thoughts and opinions about me. Would You please show me one area where I have looked for identity in the expressions of the flesh?"

Expressions of the flesh can look like performance, heritage, physical appearance, etc. What does He show you? Write it below.

_____
_____
_____
_____
_____
_____

Does He remind you of a past event? Who was involved in this event? Write your answers below.

_____
_____
_____
_____
_____
_____

What lie did you believe because you relied on your flesh to tell you who you are? Write it below.

_____
_____
_____
_____
_____

## JESUS THE FILLER OF OUR NEEDS | WORKING IT OUT

"Father God, I forgive the following people . . ."

_____
_____
_____
_____

"Lord, I repent for these unrighteous responses . . ."

_____
_____
_____
_____

"I renounce this lie . . ."

_____
_____
_____
_____

"I declare God's truth . . ."

_____
_____
_____
_____

## 4. A FALSE IDENTITY ORIGINATING FROM THE TRADITIONS OF MEN

Start off by praying this prayer: "Father God, have I entertained the traditions of men concerning who I am as a person or as Your child? Have I believed I am a sinner who is saved rather than a beloved, forgiven saint? Have I believed I am worthless, dirt, or a slave instead of a special, holy child of God?"

What does He show you? Write it below.

_____

_____

_____

_____

_____

Does He remind you of a past event? Who was involved in this event? Write your answers below.

_____

_____

_____

_____

_____

"I repent for believing these traditions of men and giving them room in my heart . . ."

_____

_____

_____

_____

_____

## JESUS THE FILLER OF OUR NEEDS | WORKING IT OUT

What lie did you believe because you relied on a human tradition to tell you who you are? Write it below.

_____

_____

_____

_____

"I forgive the people who taught me to believe and value these traditions of men." Write their names below and forgive them from your heart.

_____

_____

_____

_____

"Lord, I repent for these unrighteous responses . . ."

_____

_____

_____

_____

"I renounce this lie . . ."

_____

_____

_____

_____

**JESUS** THE FILLER OF OUR NEEDS | **IDENTITY**

"I declare God's truth . . ."

_____

_____

_____

_____

### 5. A FALSE IDENTITY ORIGINATING FROM OTHERS' THOUGHTS AND OPINIONS

Lies based on others' thoughts and opinions have two possible "sources." The first is speaking or thinking things about yourself that are not true. Ask the Lord, "Have I believed something about myself that isn't what You believe about me? Have I spoken it or thought it about myself, even though it is not true?"

What does He show you? Write it below.

_____

_____

_____

_____

_____

Does He remind you of a past event? Who was involved in this event? Write your answers below.

_____

_____

_____

_____

_____

## JESUS THE FILLER OF OUR NEEDS | WORKING IT OUT

What lie did you believe because you relied on yourself to tell you who you are? Write it below.

_____

_____

_____

_____

"I repent for declaring my own glory in these ways . . ."

_____

_____

_____

_____

"I renounce these lies . . ."

_____

_____

_____

_____

"I declare God's truth . . ."

_____

_____

_____

_____

## JESUS THE FILLER OF OUR NEEDS | IDENTITY

The second "source" for this type of identity lie is other people. Ask God, "Father God, have I believed the thoughts and opinions of others regarding my identity? Have I believed something about myself that isn't what You believe about me?"

What does He show you? Write it below.

_____
_____
_____
_____
_____
_____

Does He remind you of a past event? Who was involved in this event? Write your answers below.

_____
_____
_____
_____
_____
_____
_____

What lie did you believe because you relied on another person to tell you who you are? Write it below.

_____
_____
_____
_____
_____

## JESUS THE FILLER OF OUR NEEDS | WORKING IT OUT

"I repent for receiving another person's glory (thoughts and opinions) in these ways . . ."

_____
_____
_____
_____
_____
_____
_____
_____

"I renounce these lies . . ."

_____
_____
_____
_____
_____
_____
_____
_____

"I declare God's truth . . ."

_____
_____
_____
_____
_____
_____
_____

**JESUS** THE FILLER OF OUR NEEDS | **IDENTITY**

We run into trouble when we *long* for others' good opinions. It becomes very difficult to believe God because we're accepting glory from other people, and we don't even think to seek it from Him, even though He made us and knows us best (John 5:44). Ask the Lord, "Father God, is my heart set on seeking glory from other people?"

What does He show you? Write it below.

___

Does He remind you of a past event? Who was involved in this event? Write your answers below.

___

What lie did you believe because you longed for someone else to tell you who you are? Write it below.

___

**JESUS** THE FILLER OF OUR NEEDS | **WORKING IT OUT**

"I repent for receiving another person's glory in these ways . . ."

"I renounce these lies . . ."

"I declare God's truth . . ."

## 6. A FALSE IDENTITY ORIGINATING FROM TRAUMATIC EVENTS

After running from Pharaoh, Moses took on the identity of a sojourner—someone who is just passing through and isn't a part of the family. That was how he began to see himself because of a traumatic event (see Exodus 2:21–22). Ask the Lord, "Father God, have difficult or traumatic events negatively influenced how I see myself?"

What does He show you? Write it below.

_____

_____

_____

_____

_____

_____

Does He remind you of a past event? Who was involved in this event? Write your answers below.

_____

_____

_____

_____

_____

What lie did you believe because of this traumatic event? Write it below.

_____

_____

_____

_____

**JESUS** THE FILLER OF OUR NEEDS | **WORKING IT OUT**

"I repent for these ungodly responses . . ."

_____
_____
_____
_____
_____

"I forgive these instigators . . ."

_____
_____
_____
_____
_____

"I renounce these lies . . ."

_____
_____
_____
_____

"I declare God's truth . . ."

_____
_____
_____
_____

## 7. A FALSE IDENTITY ORIGINATING FROM THE DESIRE TO BE SEEN

You were wonderfully made to find your identity in Christ Jesus. He is the God who sees you (Genesis 16:13). Ask the Lord, "Have I sought to be seen by people rather than being passionate for Jesus to be seen in and through me?"

What does He show you? Write it below.

_____

_____

_____

_____

_____

Does He remind you of a past event? Who was involved in this event? Write your answers below.

_____

_____

_____

_____

_____

Did any sins of omission help instigate this desire to be seen by others? (A sin of omission is when the words of affirmation and blessing you needed weren't given to you.)

_____

_____

_____

_____

_____

## JESUS THE FILLER OF OUR NEEDS | WORKING IT OUT

What lie did you believe that resulted in this deep desire to be seen by others? Write it below.

_____
_____
_____
_____
_____

"I renounce this lie . . ."

_____
_____
_____
_____
_____

"I declare God's truth . . ."

_____
_____
_____
_____
_____

**CONFESS THE FOLLOWING ALOUD:**

By God's grace, I will not let traditions of men, religious traditions, verbal curses from others, verbal curses from myself, words that were not spoken but should have been, words that were spoken and should not have been, and traumatic events establish my identity. I will let only His truth establish my identity.

# THE FULLNESS OF CHRIST

When Adam and Eve sinned, it released the effects of sin and death into the fabric of humanity. Soulish needs began to manifest in people's lives, beginning with Adam and Eve and continuing down through their descendants, generation after generation.

The main nine needs are love, identity, acceptance, worth, intimacy, purpose, security, forgiveness, and the need to be needed. These needs affect all of us in one way or another, but praise God—Jesus' work on the cross dealt with the effects of sin and death. His resurrection released newness of life to us. Through Him, we receive what we desperately need in order to be whole. The Holy Spirit takes of all the fullness of Jesus Christ—even the many, many things we feel we don't deserve—and imparts it to us.

You and I have the fullness of Christ. He is our hope. He is "Christ in us, the hope of glory," and we employ His fullness in our life through faith. *That* is our reality. We start having problems only when our faith begins to drain because of worry, doubt, and unbelief. The world and our adversary work to keep us in a state of spiritual poverty, but that is not who we are. We were created to live in the abundance and light of God.

Hopefully, this workbook has helped you identify the key areas in your life where the enemy is trying to hold you captive—things that hinder your faith and keep you from accessing the fullness of Jesus Christ, which is *right here* waiting for you.

Therefore, since we have so great a cloud of witnesses surrounding us, let us also lay aside every encumbrance and the sin which so easily entangles us, and let us run with endurance the race that is set before us, fixing our eyes on Jesus, the author and perfecter of faith.

—HEBREWS 12:1–2

I have been in ministry since the late 1980s, and I've watched a whole lot of "theological fads" come and go in the body of Christ. One thing that will never fade away is our need for the fullness of Jesus and the identity He gives our soul.

# BIBLIOGRAPHY

Lucado, Max. *You Are Special.* Wheaton, IL: Crossway, 1997.

Zodhiates, Spiros. *The Complete Word Study Dictionary: New Testament* (electronic ed.). Chattanooga, TN: AMG Publishers, 2000.

# NOTES

# JESUS THE FILLER OF OUR NEEDS | NOTES

**JESUS** THE FILLER OF OUR NEEDS | **NOTES**

## JESUS THE FILLER OF OUR NEEDS | NOTES

Made in the USA
Middletown, DE
01 April 2024

52384984R10051